Basics

Beading

Opening a loop or jump ring

Because wire gets brittle if it's worked too much, handle it as little as possible.   
1 Hold the loop or jump ring with two pairs of chainnose pliers or chainnose and roundnose pliers, as shown.
2 To open the loop or jump ring, bring one pair of pliers toward you and push the other pair away.
3 String materials on the open loop or jump ring. Reverse the steps to close the open loop or jump ring.

Making a plain loop

1 Trim the wire or head pin 3/8 in. (1cm) above the top bead. Make a right angle bend close to the bead.
2 Grab the wire's tip with roundnose pliers. Roll the wire to form a half circle. Release the wire.
3 Reposition the pliers in the loop and continue rolling.
4 The finished loop should form a centered circle above the bead.

Overhand knot

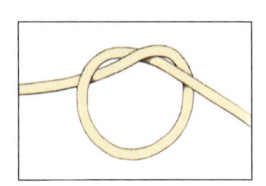

Make a loop and pass the working end through it. Pull the ends to tighten the knot.

Sewing & embroidery

Backstitch

Bring the needle up at 1. Insert the needle down through the fabric at 2, and bring it out again at 3. Pull the thread through to leave a single stitch. Repeat, keeping stitches the same length.

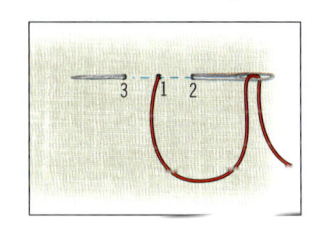

Featherstitch

Come up at 1. Insert the needle at 2. Bring the needle back out at 3, keeping the thread under the needle to form a loop. Alternate the stitches back and forth, working downward. Finish the last stitch by taking the needle back through the fabric. Secure the thread to the back.

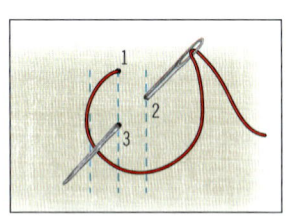

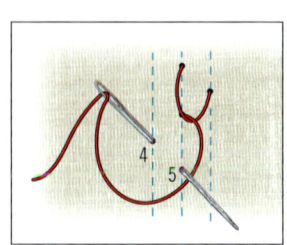

Fly stitch

Bring the needle up at 1. Insert the needle in the fabric at 2. Bring the needle back out at 3, keeping the ribbon under the needle to form a loop. Insert the needle at 4.

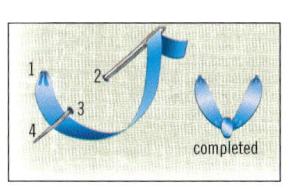

Lazy daisy stitch

Come up through the fabric at 1 and form a loop. Go down at 2, close to 1. Next, bring the needle up at 3 to catch the ribbon loop. Make sure the ribbon is not twisted and anchor the loop at 4.

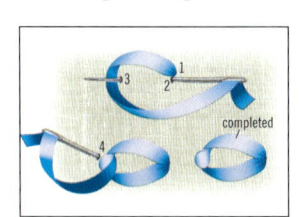

Running stitch

Bring the needle up through the fabric at 1, and down through the fabric at 2. Repeat, keeping stitches even.

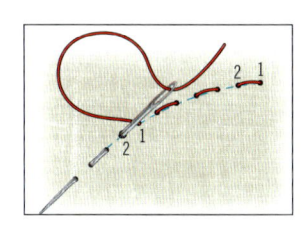

Straight stitch

Come up at 1 and go down at 2, making the stitch the desired length.

Stem stitch

Bring the needle up through the fabric at 1. The needle is inserted to the right of the line at 2 and brought up to the left of the line at 3, making a thick outline.

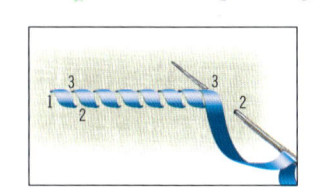

Whipstitch

Whipstitch is used to hand-sew seams. Bring the needle through the material on the bottom side of the opening and push it through the material on the upper side of the opening at an angle, as shown. Repeat to close the opening.

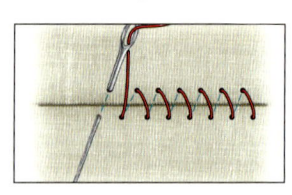

Threading a needle with ribbon

1 Cut the end at a 45-degree angle. Thread the cut end through the needle.
2 Secure ribbon on needle by running the needle through the ribbon about ⅛ in. (3mm) from the cut end. Pull the long end of the ribbon through the eye, sliding the cut end down to the eye of the needle.

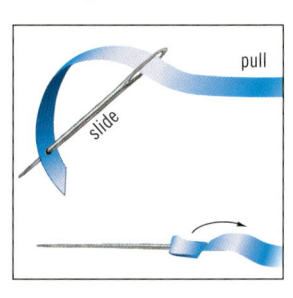

Knotting the ribbon end

1 Fold the loose end of the ribbon over ¼ in. (6mm).
2 Push the needle through both thicknesses of the folded ribbon.
3 Pull the needle all the way through the ribbon, forming a knot at the end of the ribbon length.

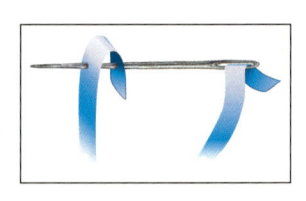

Family frame

Use beads in conjunction with scrapbooking supplies to create this easy frame.

[1] Cover the frame with cardstock. Adhere the front portion of an old greeting card at an angle in the upper left-hand corner. Place a sticker in the lower right-hand corner.
[2] Trim a photo to approximately 5 x 7 in. (12.7 x 17.8cm). Round two corners of the photo, and use a scissors to distress the photo's edges. Adhere the photo to the cardstock-covered frame at an angle, overlapping the greeting card. Glue a metal photo corner to the photo's upper right corner, and place a sticker over the photo's rounded upper left corner. Place the flower at the top of the photo, and secure the flower center with a brad.
[3] Place double-sided tape across the frame, about ½ in. (1.3cm) from the bottom. Sprinkle a mix of seed beads and glitter over the tape; press firmly with your fingers to secure. Shake off the excess beads and glitter, and cover the beaded mix with Glossy Accents for a permanent hold.
[4] Cut 1 yd. (.9m) of embroidery floss. Wrap it around the frame three times, overlapping the bottom of the photo. Secure the floss to the back with an overhand knot (Basics, p. 3). Use a dimensional adhesive to attach the "love" tag over the center of the wrapped floss.
[5] Rub an ink pad along the edges of the frame.
[6] Secure the completed frame to the base. ● – *May Flaum*

MATERIALS

- 8 x 10 in. (20 x 25cm) frame and base (Me and My Big Ideas)
- cardstock (Bazzill Basics)
- double-sided tape
- dimensional adhesive
- Glossy Accents (Ranger)
- ink to complement cardstock (Distress Ink: Ranger)
- "baby," "family," and "remember" stickers (Creative Imaginations)
- "love" tag (Me and My Big Ideas)
- flower embellishment (Making Memories)
- brad
- metal photo corner (Making Memories)
- recycled greeting card
- assorted seed beads to match cardstock
- glitter
- embroidery floss

Bead and chain frame

Delicate cable chain and beaded head pins add style to a plain wooden frame.

[1] Disassemble the frame, removing the glass and backing materials.

[2] Working with the frame's 5-in. (12.7cm) edges as top and bottom, measure in ½ in. (1.3cm) from each corner and mark the spot along the bottom edge of the frame. Measure the center points along the top and bottom edges, and mark the spots on the back of the frame.

[3] Use an awl to create a starter hole at each mark. Insert an eye screw into each hole along the bottom of the frame. Use a screw to attach the toggle bar to the top center of the frame.

[4] Slide the hooked 3-in-1 connector through the center eye screw along the bottom of the frame. Open two jump rings (Basics, p. 3), slide a connector on each, and attach a completed unit to the remaining eye screws along the frame's bottom. Close the jump rings.

[5] Cut two 4-in. (10cm) and one 8-in. (20cm) pieces of chain and open six jump rings. Slide a jump ring onto each end of each piece of chain. Attach one end of a 4-in. chain to the right hole on the left connector, and attach the other end to the left hole on the center connector. Attach the other 4-in. chain in the same manner, with one jump ring through the right hole of the center connector and the other through the left hole of the right connector. Repeat to attach the 8-in. chain, with one end connected to the center hole of the left connector and the other connected to the center hole in the right connector.

[6] String three head pins in the following pattern: seed bead, glass bead, seed bead, glass bead, seed bead, glass bead, seed bead. Make a plain loop (Basics) at the top of each head pin.

[7] Open the loop on one beaded head pin, and attach the head pin to the center hole on the center connector. Attach the remaining head pins to the outermost holes of the connectors to the left and right of the frame in the same manner.

[8] Replace the glass, add a photo to the frame, and replace the backing materials. – *Lorine Mason*

MATERIALS

- 3 x 5 in. (7.6 x 12.7cm) wooden photo frame
- toggle bar
- 3 3-in-1 connectors (one with hook)
- 16 in. (41cm) 2mm cable chain (Beadalon)
- chainnose pliers (Beadalon)
- roundnose pliers
- wire cutters (Beadalon)
- 6 6mm jump rings (Beadalon)
- assorted glass and seed beads (Beadalon)
- 3 2-in. (5cm) head pins (Beadalon)
- 3 eye screws
- ruler & pencil
- awl
- screwdriver
- small screw

Easy wire photo holder

Highlight a simple wire holder with foil-lined glass beads.

Make the bottom

[1] Cut 17 in. (43cm) of wire. String the two identical beads to the center.

[2] Using your fingers and chainnose pliers, shape one end of the wire into a spiral or square. Then, shape the other end of the wire to be the mirror image of the first.

[3] To harden and flatten the wire, lay one end on a steel block and hammer the design with a ball peen hammer (**photo a**). Be sure to hammer only the part of the wire that has been shaped. Repeat on the other end.

[4] Because the beads are thick, you need to shape the wire around the bead to lie flat against the plastic holder. First, lay the design flat against the work surface. Then, bend the wire straight up at a right angle to the design. Slide one of the beads next to the design, and gently bend the wire so that the bead sits flat next to the design. Repeat on the other side.

[5] Bend the wire at a right angle to the bead on the other side so the wire is parallel to the bend in step 4. Using chainnose pliers, bend the wire at the edge of the bead so that it is once again parallel to the design and the bead (**photo b**). This should be a snug fit. Repeat on the other side.

[6] Measure to find the halfway point on the wire. Match this point to the halfway point on the photo frame. With the center points aligned, mark the edges of the photo frame on the wire (**photo c**).

[7] Grasp the mark on the wire with the widest part of your roundnose pliers. Bend the wire around the pliers so that it is parallel to the bead and the design (**photo d**). Repeat on the other side.

[8] Slide the bottom portion of the photo holder onto the frame (**photo e**). If the fit is loose, use your chainnose pliers to pinch the corners together.

Make the top

[1] Cut 17 in. of wire. String the remaining bead to the center of the wire.

[2] Bend both ends of the wire at a right angle to the bead (**photo f**).

[3] Place the bead where you want it to sit on the photo holder. Mark the end of the holder on the wire.

[4] Use your roundnose pliers to bend the wire back on itself, as in step 7 above. Slide the bead unit back onto the photo holder, and check that it will fit securely (**photo g**). If it doesn't, remove the bead unit from the holder and compress the bend with your chainnose pliers. Check the fit again.

[5] Bend the ends of the wires out at a 45-degree angle. Make a second bend on each wire 3½-4 in. (8.3-10cm) below the first. Gently bend these two wires away from each other.

[6] Slide the plastic photo holder out of the bottom of the wire frame. Where the wire ends meet the wire that runs above the bottom of the holder, bend the ends up and around the wire, forming a loop. Trim the excess wire. Slide your photo into the plastic holder, and then slide the plastic holder into the wire frame (**photo h**). –*Lesley Weiss*

MATERIALS

- 34 in. (86cm) 16-gauge craft wire
- 3 foil-lined glass beads:
  2 1 x 1 x .5 in. (identical or complementary)
  1 1 x .5 x .5 in.
- 4 x 6 in. (10 x 15cm) plastic photo holder
- roundnose pliers
- chainnose pliers
- wire cutters
- marker
- steel block
- ball peen hammer

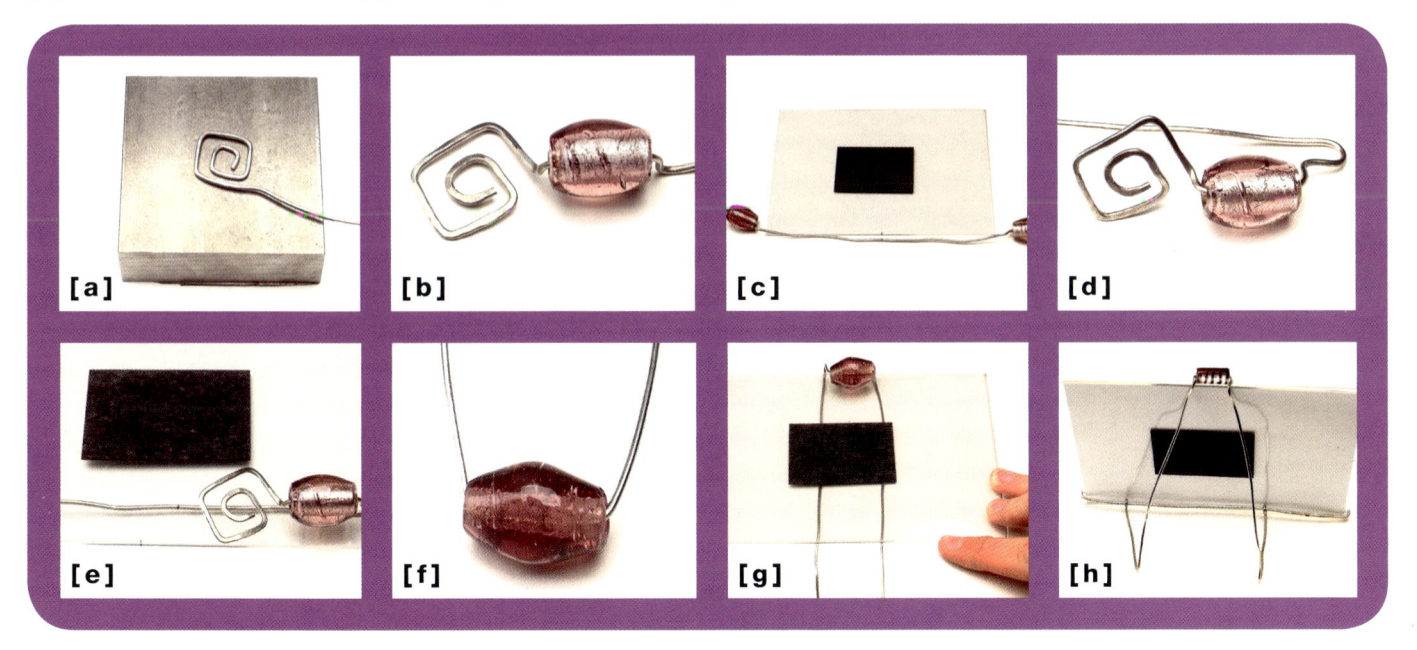

Freeform wire frame

Embellish a curved wire frame with beads and contrasting wire.

Make the frame

[1] On a piece of paper, trace around the outside of the photo holder with a marker. Determine how wide you want the frame to be, and draw another rectangle to those dimensions around the first.

[2] Using your roundnose pliers, turn a large loop at one end of the 16-gauge wire. Using the tracing as a guide, use roundnose pliers and your fingers to shape the wire into curves, loops, and coils. Keep the overall shape within the tracing, and take care to keep the edges square (photo a).

[3] When your design reaches all the way around your tracing, make another loop to fit tightly around the first (photo b). Slide the photo holder into the design and check to make sure it will sit evenly. If needed, adjust the shape by pulling the curves apart or pushing them together.

[4] Place the rectangle on a steel block and hammer the curves (photo c). This will harden the frame, helping it to maintain its shape. Do not hammer where the wire crosses over itself.

[5] Cut a 5-in. (12.7cm) piece of 22-gauge wire. Put one end through the overlapped loops. Begin tightly wrapping the wire around both loops, binding them together and forming a tight, uniform coil around the wires (photo d). Trim the excess wire and press the cut edges against the back of the piece.

8 Beaded Photo Frames

Make the corner braces

[1] Cut four 5-in. pieces and four 4-in. pieces of 22-gauge wire.

[2] Choose four points in each inside corner where you will attach the wire. Place the frame and the wires on top of the photo holder, to check where each wire will lay (**photo e**). The outside (4-in.) wires should cross the tips of each corner on the plastic holder, while the inside (5-in.) wires cross the corners about ½ in. inside. Mark the wire frame where the braces will sit.

[3] Attach the outside coils first. Using chainnose pliers and your fingers, tightly coil one end of a 4-in. wire four times around the frame where marked. Pull the tail across the top of the frame to the opposite point on the corner. Make sure all the outer corner braces cross the top of the frame, so that they will fit OVER the photo holder corners. Coil the other end of the wire around the frame wire four times (**photo f**). Do not pull the corners too tightly, or the frame will be distorted. Trim the excess wire and press the cut edges against the back of the frame. Repeat in the remaining corners.

[4] Attach the 5-in. pieces of wire to the inner marks on each corner of the frame in the same way you connected the outside wires (**photo g**). The inside wires should cross the corners on the back of the frame, so that they will fit UNDER the photo holder corners.

[5] Check the fit of the frame around the photo holder. If necessary, adjust the fit of the frame by gently pulling the curves apart or pushing them together. (If the wire has been hammered, it will become brittle if you adjust it too much.)

Add the beads

[1] Lay the frame on a flat surface and decide where to place your beads. Smaller beads will fit into the curves of the frame, while larger beads might sit on an outside edge or on top of a coil.

[2] Cut a 5-in. piece of 26-gauge copper wire. Starting at the center, coil the copper wire around the frame wire next to where you want to attach your first bead. When you like the length of the coil, string the bead on the wire and coil the tails around the next curve (**photo h**).

[3] Continue adding beads around the frame. You can vary the length of the coils, or connect a series of beads by using longer wires. Make sure you press all the ends against the back of the frame.

Make the frame stand

[1] Cut a 9-in. (23cm) piece of 16-gauge wire.

[2] Using your roundnose pliers, bend the wire at a 45-degree angle 4 in. from one end.

[3] Use roundnose pliers to create hooks, pointing inward, on either end of the wire.

[4] Slide the hook on the longer end of the wire onto a lower curve near the center of the top of the frame (**photo i**).

[5] Slide the other hook onto an upper curve near the center of the bottom of the frame (**photo j**). Press each hook closed around the wire. – *Lesley Weiss*

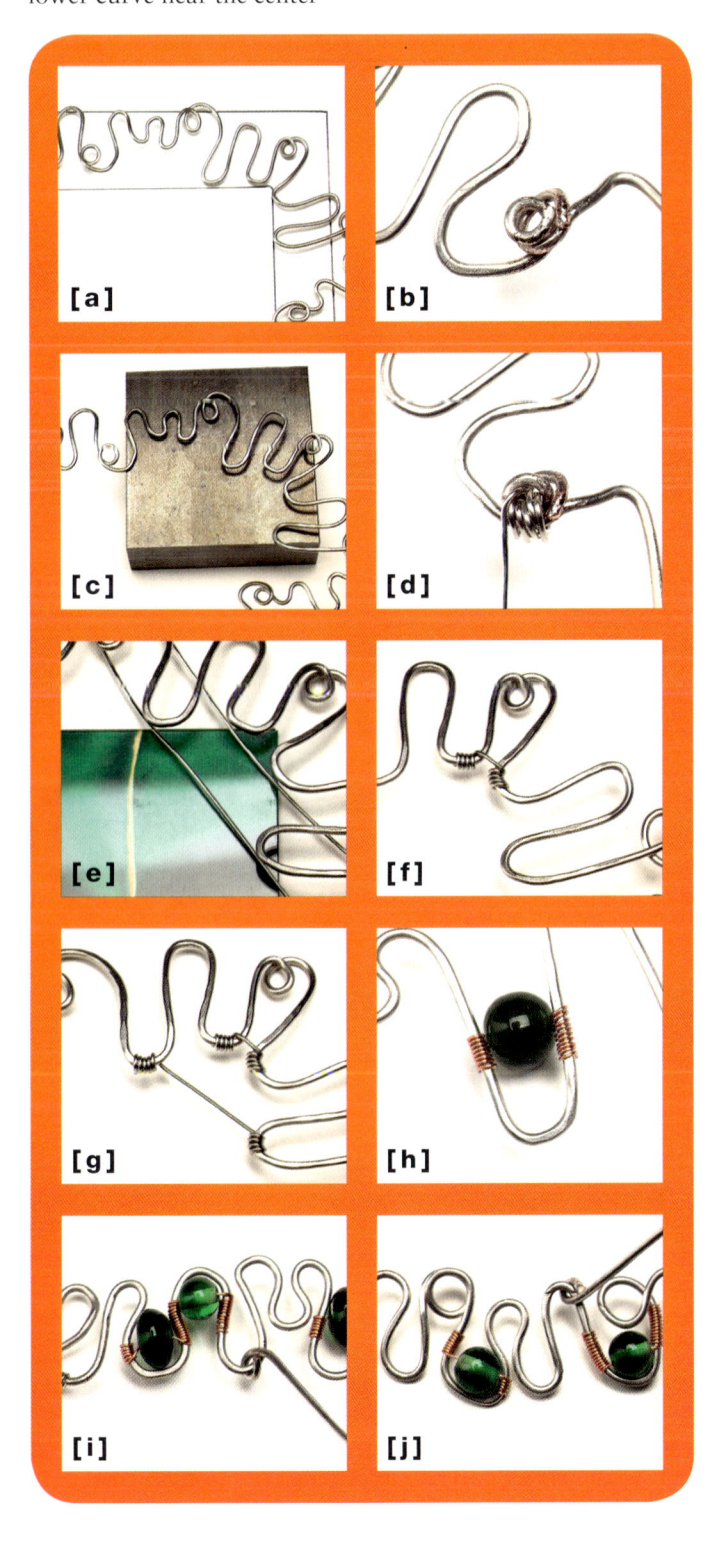

MATERIALS

- 30-40 in. (.76-1.1m) 16-gauge craft wire, silver
- spool 26-gauge craft wire, copper
- 24 in. (61cm) 22-gauge craft wire, silver
- 25-50 assorted glass beads
- 4 x 6 in. (10 x 15cm) plastic photo holder
- roundnose pliers
- chainnose pliers
- wire cutters
- paper
- marker
- steel block
- ball peen hammer

[a] [b] [c] [d] [e] [f] [g] [h] [i] [j]

Beaded Photo Frames

Painting with beads

Use a simple "painting with beads" technique for a frame that recalls the colors and landscapes of the American Southwest.

[1] Draw the frame's outline on tracing paper. Decide beforehand if you want to use the frame for a photograph or a mirror. If you plan to frame a photograph, consider a less complex design, so the frame will not compete with the photograph. In planning your frame, be sure to continue elements from one side to the other to provide balance. If you've chosen lots of dark beads, such as purples, blues, and blacks, for the design, consider painting your frame black.

[2] If you wish, use wood cut-out elements of animals, plants or trees, mountains, and clouds to give the design dimension. Draw and cut each design out of ¼-in. (6mm) pine with a scroll saw. (If you have no access to woodworking tools, look in craft-supply stores. They have large selections of pre-cut wood shapes that can be incorporated into your design.)

[3] Once you've drawn your design and decided where to place any cut-outs, back the tracing paper with carbon paper and trace it on the frame (**photo a**). If your frame is a dark color, use white carbon paper.

[4] Start by beading all the cut-out elements. Cover a small area (about five or six bead lengths) with Gem-Tac adhesive, then pick up each bead individually with dental tweezers. Position the bead with the tweezers and use the excavator spoon shank to tap the bead into place. Within each element of the design, try to keep the beads aligned in rows so their holes are oriented in the same direction. Also, because beads vary slightly in size, look for smaller beads that you can fit into any gaps in the beading.

[5] Once all the cut-out elements are covered, begin beading the frame using the techniques described in step 4 (**photo b**). Work from left to right, following the design. Use bugle beads to accent sharp lines in the design and to outline the edge of the frame.

[6] When you are within a few beads of the location of a cut-out element, use Aleene's wood glue to cement the cut-out in position (**photo c**). Then finish beading up to the element and continue on the other side.

[7] After you have completed the entire frame, look over the work and fit small beads into any obvious gaps that may exist in the design. ○ – *Claudia Cattell*

MATERIALS
- flat, wide, wood frame
- assorted seed beads, bugle beads, crystals, and rhinestones in a palette suited to your design
- tracing paper
- carbon paper
- Gem-Tac permanent adhesive
- Aleene's wood glue
- wood cut-outs (cut your own from ¼-in./6mm pine or buy them at craft-supply stores)
- dental tweezers
- excavator spoon shank (available at dental and scientific supply shops)

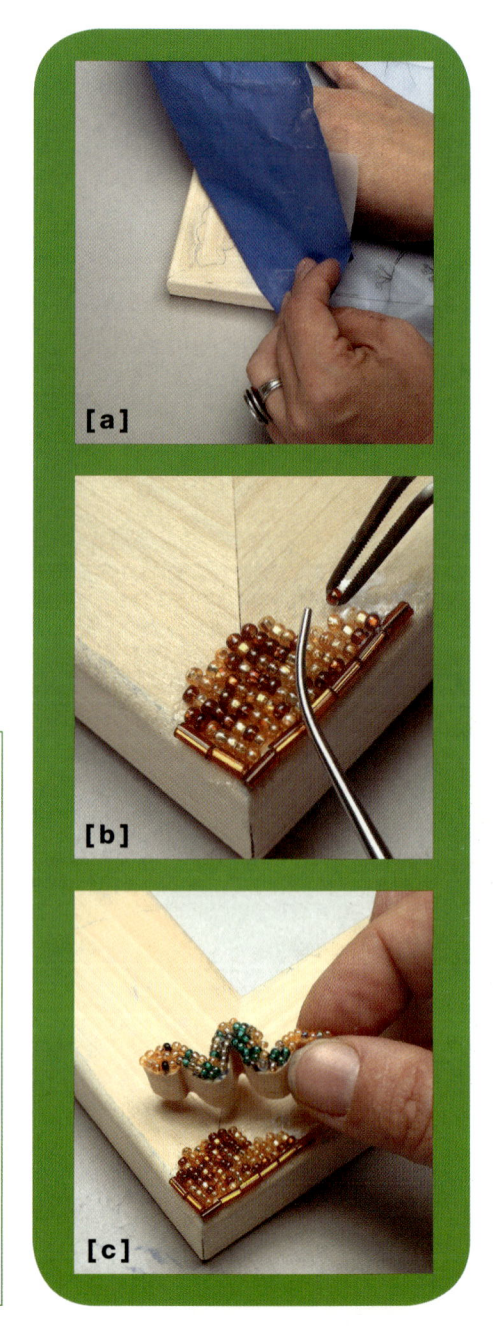

[a]

[b]

[c]

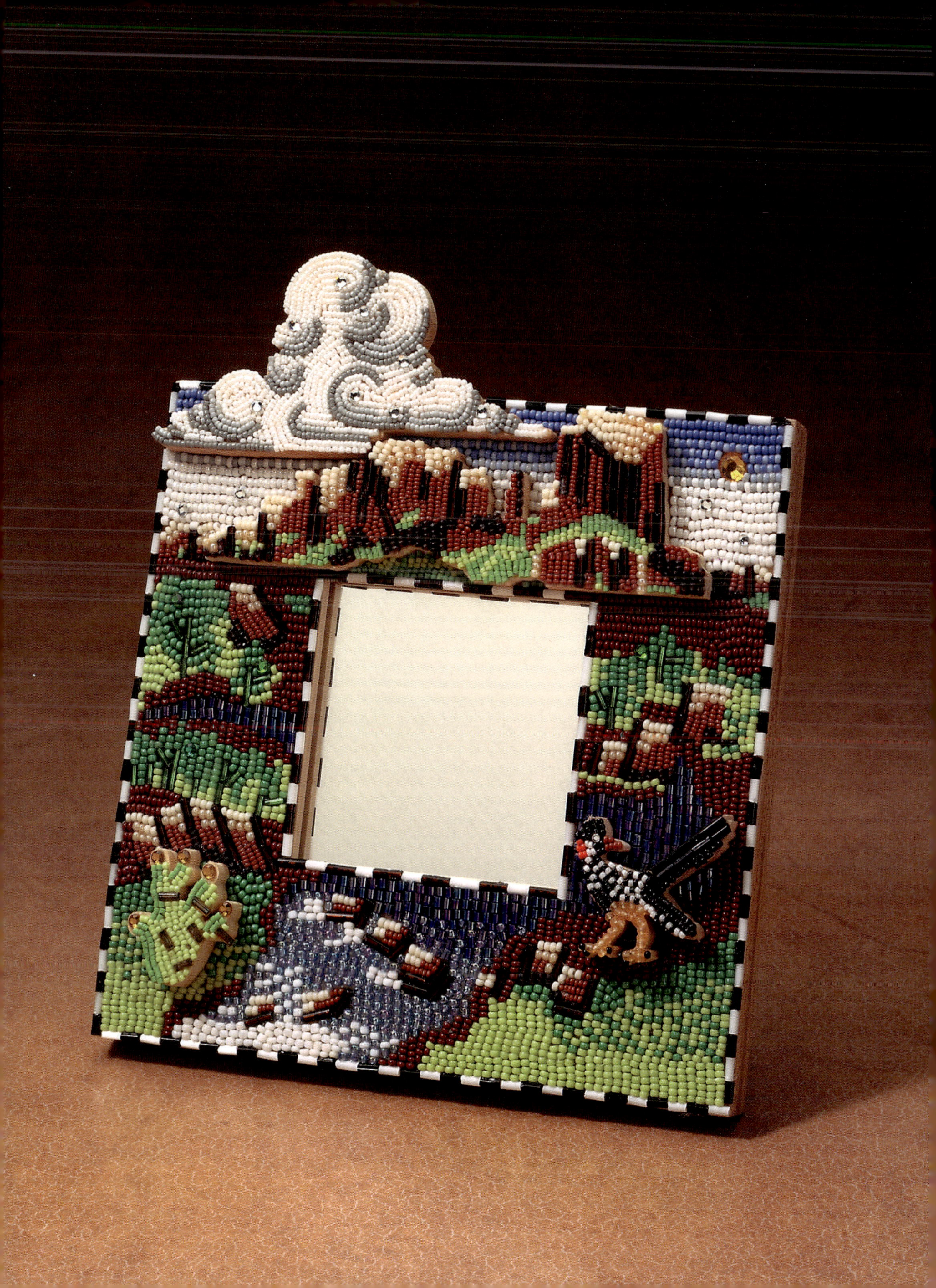

Ribbon rose frame

Add a rosy ambience to any room with this elegant embroidered frame.

[1] Place the mat board in the center of the fabric piece. Trace the outline and opening of the mat board using an air-soluble fabric pen.

MATERIALS

- 6½ x 8½ in. (16.5 x 22cm) piece of pink and white cotton fabric
- 5 x 7 in. (12.7 x 17.8cm) mat frame with 3 x 4½ in. (7.6 x 11.4cm) oval opening
- 5 x 7 in. piece of batting
- 5 x 7 in. photo frame to match fabric
- hand-dyed silk ribbon in 7mm Variegated Green, #012 (YLI Corp.)
- 1 yd. (.9m) 4mm Light Green #18 silk ribbon in (YLI Corp.)
- 10 in. (25cm) 7mm Medium Coral #24 silk ribbon (YLI Corp.)
- 10 in. 7mm Magenta #145 silk ribbon (YLI Corp.)
- ½ yd. (46cm) 13mm Pink Violet #144 silk ribbon (YLI Corp.)
- 2 colors embroidery floss (Light Gray Green #524 and Fern Green #320: DMC)
- khaki satin and light beige pearl seed beads, size 10º (Firefly Beadcrafts)
- embroidery needle
- beading needle
- beading thread
- fabric glue
- scissors
- ruler
- tape
- tracing paper
- pencil
- light table
- air-soluble fabric pen

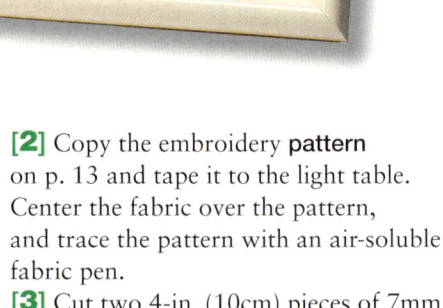

[2] Copy the embroidery **pattern** on p. 13 and tape it to the light table. Center the fabric over the pattern, and trace the pattern with an air-soluble fabric pen.

[3] Cut two 4-in. (10cm) pieces of 7mm magenta ribbon and one 4-in. piece of 7mm medium coral ribbon. Stitch a running stitch along the edge of one magenta ribbon (**figure 1**). Pull the thread to gather the ribbon into a flower (**figure 2**). Make another magenta flower and a coral flower.

[4] Cut 3½ in. (8.xcm) of 13mm pink violet ribbon. Tie a loose overhand knot (Basics, p. 3) in the center of the ribbon for the bud, and tie another overhand knot on top of the first one (**figure 3**). Pull the ribbon ends together and wrap a 3-in. 7.6cm) piece of green ribbon around the knot, crossing over in the front (**figure 4**). Use needle and thread

12 Beaded Photo Frames

PATTERN

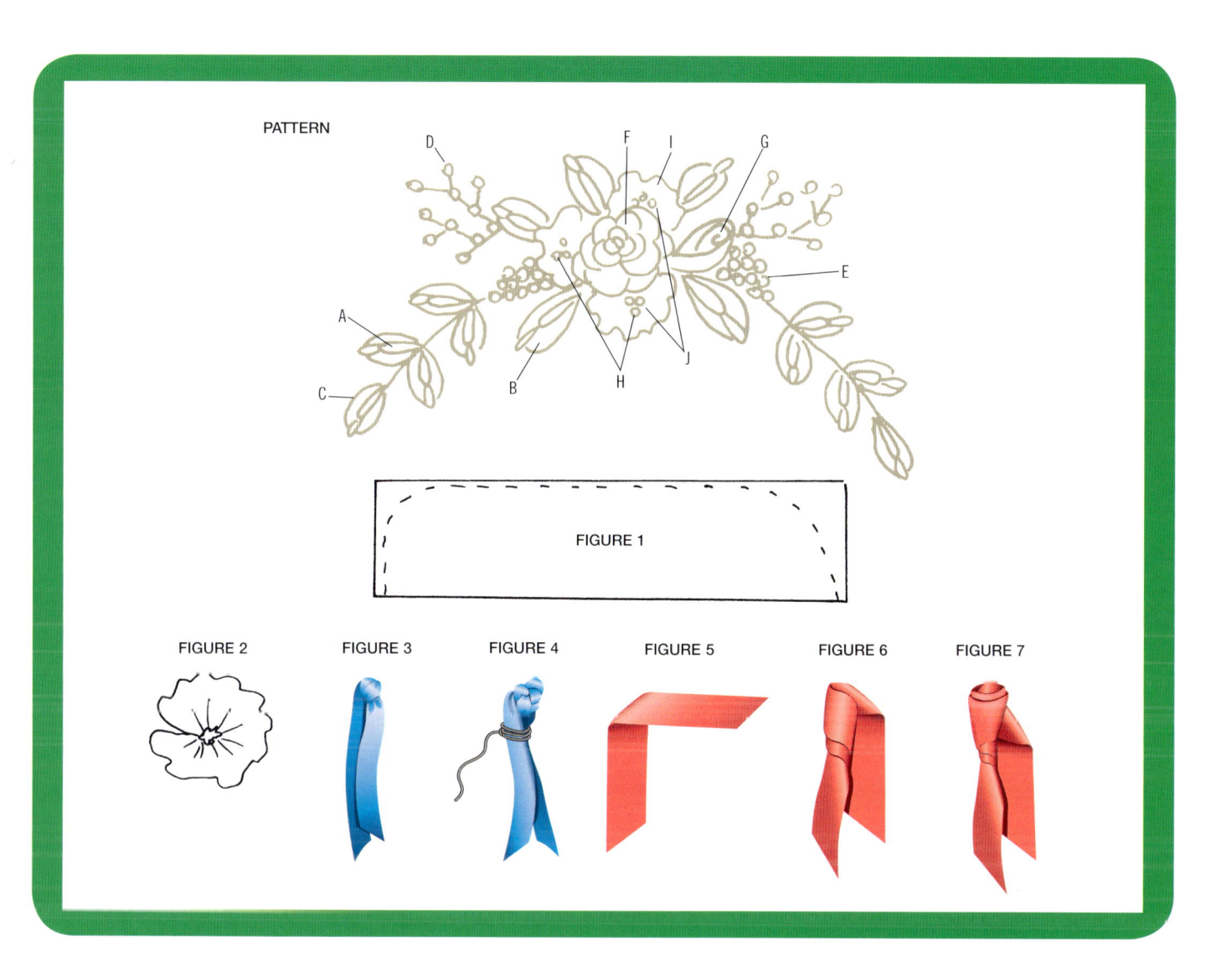

FIGURE 1

FIGURE 2   FIGURE 3   FIGURE 4   FIGURE 5   FIGURE 6   FIGURE 7

to secure all the ribbon ends, and trim the excess ribbon.

[5] Cut 7 in. (17.8cm) of 13mm pink violet ribbon. Fold the ribbon over at the corner (**figure 5**) and roll the ribbon end several times to cover the folded edge (**figure 6**). Thread the sewing needle, and stitch the coil securely so it does not unfold. Turn the top of ribbon away from the coil, and roll the center coil (**figure 7**). Roll the ribbon bud onto the folded length; stitch securely at the base and sides. Continue to turn, roll, and stitch until the rose is the desired size. Tuck the ribbon end under, and secure it to the back of the rose.

[6] Embroider the pattern on the fabric, using the stitch guide at right (see Basics for stitches). Add beads using a beading needle and beading thread.

[7] Starting 1/8 in. (3mm) from the outside edge of the traced opening, use an air-soluble fabric pen to mark the fabric every 1/4 in. (6mm). Sew a pearl seed bead over each mark.

[8] Glue the batting to the front of the mat board. Trim the edges and cut out the opening. Center the fabric over the mat board. Fold the fabric on the outside edges to the back and tape in place. Pull the fabric corners toward the center and tape down. Cut the center opening and trim to 3/4 in. (9mm) from the edges of the mat board. Clip the fabric around the curve of the oval on the inside of the frame. Pull the edge fabric to the back, and tape in place. ○

– Denise Giles

Stitch guide

A. Stem stitch the stem using two strands of fern green embroidery floss.
B. Lazy daisy stitch large leaves using 7mm variegated green silk ribbon.
C. Lazy daisy stitch small leaves using 4mm light green silk ribbon.
D. Backstitch baby's breath stems using one strand of light gray green embroidery floss. Sew a pearl seed bead to the end of each stem.
E. Sew clusters of khaki satin seed beads.
F. Attach the stitched rose.
G. Attach the rosebud.
H. Attach two magenta gathered roses.
I. Attach the medium coral gathered rose.
J. Sew three pearl seed beads in the center of each gathered rose.

Beaded Photo Frames 13

Gold mat frame

Enhance a plain gold photo frame with beaded ribbon embroidery against a silk background.

[1] Cut a 16 x 14 in. (41 x 35.5cm) piece of silk dupioni. Place the mat board on top of the fabric. Using an air-soluble fabric pen, trace the outside and opening of the mat board.

[2] Enlarge the embroidery **pattern** by 135%. Tape the pattern to a light box, place the fabric over it so the pattern falls between the openings traced in step 1, and trace the pattern onto the fabric with the air-soluble pen.

[3] Cut three 10-in. (25cm) pieces of the brown silk ribbon. Mark every 2 in. (5cm) with the air-soluble pen. Thread the needle and stitch a running stitch through the ribbon, from one end to the other (**figure 1**). Pull thread to gather the ribbon to form the petals (**figure 2**). Tack the last petal to the first, forming a circle of petals (**figure 3**). Stitch the ends to secure.

[4] Cut four 8-in. (20cm) pieces of 7mm camel silk ribbon. Stitch a running stitch (Basics, p. 3) along the edge of the ribbon (**figure 1**, p. 13). Pull the thread to gather ribbon. Sew the ends together to form a circle, and secure the stitch.

[5] Embroider the pattern to the fabric, using the stitch guide (see Basics for stitches). Attach the beads with a beading needle and beading thread.

[6] Use two 10-in. pieces of 3/8-in. wide sheer toffee ribbon for the tacked loop ribbons. Thread the ribbon onto the needle and knot one end. Come up next to the flower and twist the ribbon. With beading needle and thread, tack the ribbon down with a seed bead where it touches the fabric. Continue twisting and tacking the ribbon around the oval marking on the fabric. Remove the ribbon needle. Trim the ribbon ends and tack ½ in. (1.3cm) from each end of the ribbon with a seed bead.

[7] Spray adhesive on the mat board and press the batting into the glue. Trim any excess batting from the edges and opening. Center the embroidered fabric over the mat. Pull the fabric edges to the back and tape them in place. Cut the center opening and trim to ¾ in. from the edges of the mat board. Clip the fabric around the curve of the oval on the inside of the frame. Pull the fabric to the back and tape in place.

[8] Place the finished mat in the frame, and add the photo and backing. Tape the backing in place, and add a picture hanger to the back of the frame. ●

– Denise Giles

PATTERN

FIGURE 1

FIGURE 2

FIGURE 3

MATERIALS
- ½ yd. (44cm) gold silk dupioni fabric
- 11 x 14 in. (24 x 35.5cm) mat with 9½ x 7½ in. (24 x 19cm) opening
- batting
- 11 x 14 in. foam core board
- frame and photo
- 2 yd. (1.8m) silk ribbon (YLI Corp.) in each of the following colors:
  13mm #011 Brown (hand-dyed)
  7mm #51 Camel
  7mm #32 Med. Sage
  4mm #33 Dk. Sage
- embroidery floss (#3787 Wolf Gray: DMC)
- gold iris seed beads, size 6º (Firefly Beadcrafts)
- bronze opaque seed beads, size 10º (Firefly Beadcrafts)
- 24 in. (61cm) sheer toffee ribbon, ⅜ in. wide
- embroidery needle
- beading needle and beading thread
- tape
- picture hanging kit
- scissors
- pencil
- light box
- air-soluble fabric pen

Stitch guide
A. Straight stitch the tip of the fern and fly stitch the rest of the fern using 4mm dark sage silk ribbon.
B. Featherstitch the vine using wolf gray embroidery floss. Sew bronze seed beads at each point.
C. Lazy daisy stitch the leaves using 7mm medium sage silk ribbon.
D. Attach the brown silk flower. Sew five gold iris beads in its center.
E. Attach the camel silk flowers. Sew five bronze seed beads in the center of each.
F. Twist and tack down the sheer toffee ribbon with the gold iris beads.

Beaded Photo Frames 15

Loom-woven rainbow

Try this loom project to learn good weaving habits, handy tricks and shortcuts for color selection, split-loom weaving, and quick finishing techniques.

[a] [b] [c]

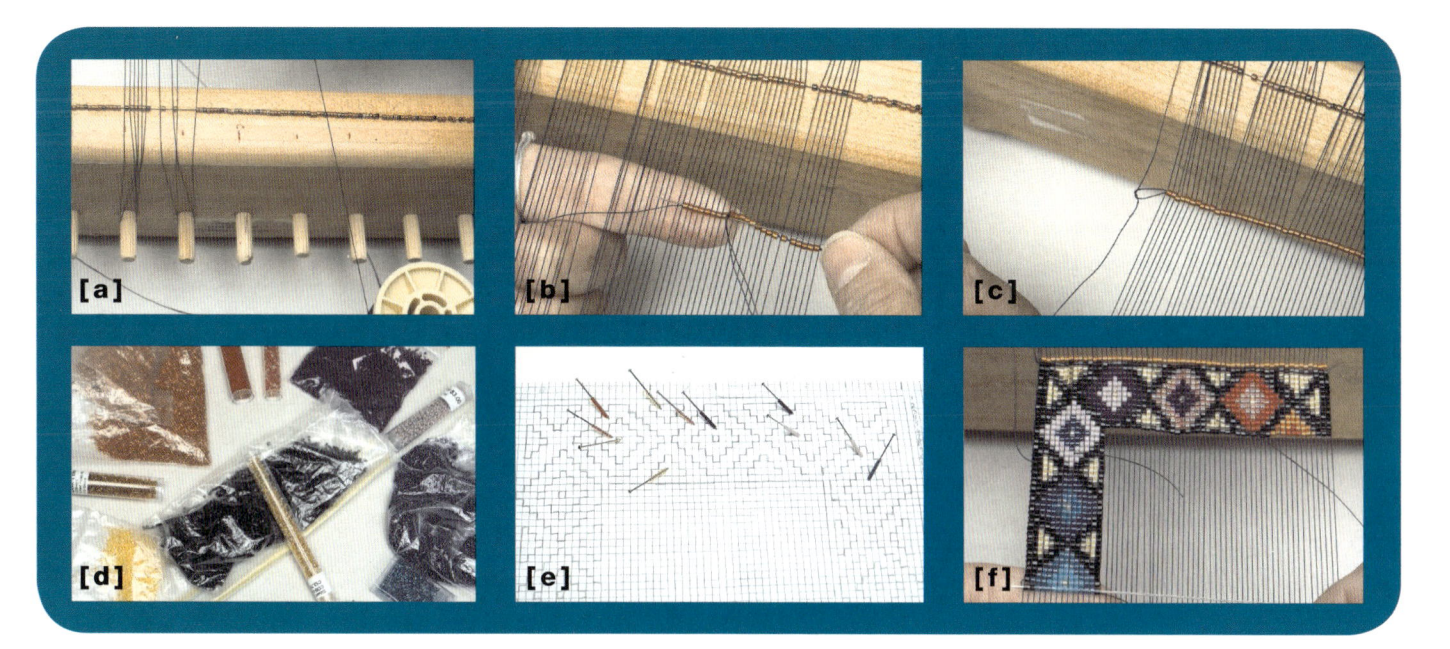

[d] [e] [f]

To make the picture or mirror frame shown above, you'll need a loom wide enough to accommodate a piece that's 3¼ in. (8.3cm) wide (60 warps) by 3⅞ in. (10cm) long. Allow extra length for the warp tails.

After warping your loom, select colors and key them onto your chart. Then weave the picture frame, starting at the top. Next, seal the warp threads and then mount the weaving to the frame.

warping

[1] To aid in warping any piece wider than 1-2 in. (2.5-5cm), place a piece of tape alongside the springs, rods, or other thread-separating devices. Figure out how wide the finished piece will be by stringing 20-30 of the seed beads you'll be using and counting the number in an inch. Then divide the number of warp threads needed by the number of beads per inch.

[2] Transfer the width measurement to the tape. Then subdivide the total measurement into fourths or more (**photo a**). Repeat on the other end of the loom. Now you know how many warps to space in each subdivision.

[3] As you string the warps, skip or double up in some spaces to make the warp come out even. Maintain a firm, even tension of all the warp threads.

After I've finished warping, I always weave a dummy row on its own length of thread before I begin my piece, using the same beads I will be using in the project. This row spaces the warps perfectly so that the weaving, which starts separately below it, can begin with precision and ease.

weaving tips

If this is a wider project than you've ever tackled before, here are some things to keep in mind:

[1] Tie your long weaving thread to the end warp on the side opposite your dominant hand (left for righties and right for lefties). Make a single knot that you can later untie to weave in the starting thread.

[2] String the correct number of beads for the dummy row (59 for this 60-warp piece) and bring the needle under all the warp threads to your dominant side. Do not try to position all of these beads between the warp threads at once. Starting at the far right (left for lefties), push up and align a few of the beads with your non-dominant index finger. Then pass the needle through these beads above the warp threads (**photo b**). Be careful not to pierce the warp threads. Don't pull the thread all the way through. Align the next small group of beads and repeat until you've gone through all the beads.

[3] Use the loop of thread and the needle end of thread to pull the row straight and gradually pull the thread all the way through the beads until it's snug. Notice how much easier it is to align your weaving with that loop. Tie the starting and ending tails together tightly against the last warp thread (**photo c**) and cut off the tails.

MATERIALS

- 2g each of 13 colors Japanese cylinder beads, size 11º: medium and dark red, purple and lavender, dark and medium blue, turquoise, dark and medium green, yellow, tan, orange, and gold
- 7g Japanese cylinder beads for background, black or white
- Silamide beading thread
- beading needles, #10 or 12 or sharps
- Big Eye needle
- ½-in.- (1.3cm) thick Foamcore
- ⅛-in.- (3mm) thick matboard
- iron-on interfacing (fabric store)
- loom that has at least 4 in. (10cm) of weaving width
- 5-in.-square (13cm) leather or Ultrasuede
- sewing pins
- steam iron and pressing mitt or pad
- 4 clothespins
- tape
- marker
- white glue

Beaded Photo Frames 17

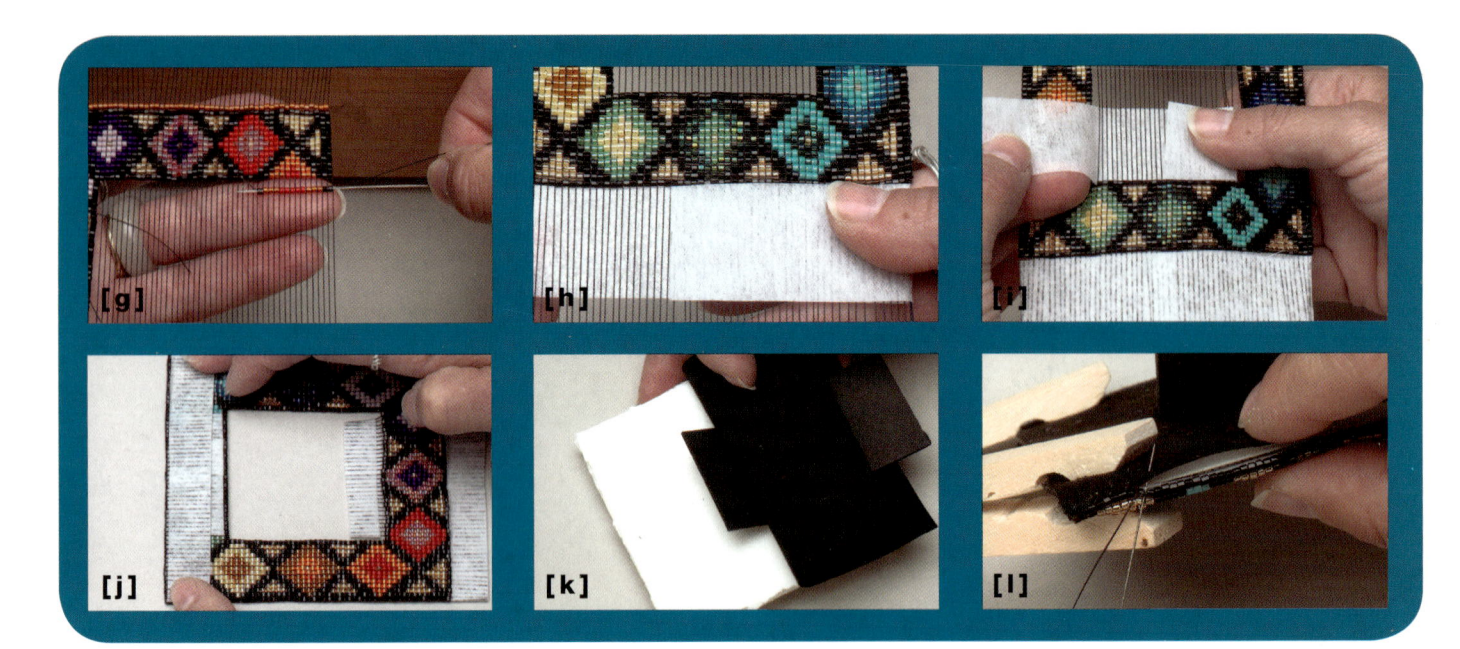

color planning

You could successfully execute this project with only two colors: one for the background and another for the diamonds and triangles. But it's fun to handle the colors of the diamonds like a color wheel, traveling from hue to hue around the frame.

[1] Find 12 colors that you like. Arrange them in a pleasing circular order. Then choose a color for the lattice background (I used black) and an accent color (I chose gold) for the triangles and diamond centers.

[2] Put the accent and background colors inside the circle or nearby (**photo d**, p. 17). Consider color intensity, light/dark values, surfaces, and finishes. Mixing matte, shiny, silver-lined, luster, and hex in the same piece will add richness and texture.

[3] When you are satisfied with your color layout, use the following shortcut to get right to the weaving. It bypasses coloring your chart but allows you to keep track of which beads go where.
a. Enlarge the black and white chart at right by 115% and tape it to a ½-in.-thick (1.3cm) sheet of Foamcore.
b. Starting with the first of your 12 colors, place five or six beads on a straight sewing pin and poke it through the outer section of the first diamond at an angle so you can see the color.
c. Put a pin of color 2 beads into the inner section of the first diamond and the outer section of the second. Carry on in this manner in a clockwise direction around the frame (**photo e**, p. 17). You'll end up putting color 1 in the inner section of the last diamond.
d. Use the accent color for the diamond centers and the triangles.

weaving

I always start weaving at the top of the loom and work the rows toward myself. As I complete a row, I draw a light pencil line through it.
[1] Weave rows 1-13 to complete the top of the frame.

[2] Continue with the same thread or weave in a new thread by beginning it several rows back and weaving back and forth through a few beads at a time until the needle emerges at the old thread. Weave rows 14-44 on the left side of the frame if you're a rightie or on the right side of the frame if you're a leftie. On each of these rows, string the 14 beads below the warps. Bring your needle back up to the top between the 15th and 16th warps from the edge you're weaving (photo f) and pass back through the beads above the warps.

[3] Wind up any remaining weaving thread after row 44 and temporarily tape or fasten it out of the way.

[4] To begin the other side, tie a new length of weaving thread to the 15th warp from the other edge. Pass it under the warp threads and string the beads for row 14. Then weave back through the beads above the warps toward the middle of the frame (photo g). Continue through row 44 on this side, always passing down between warps 15 and 16.

[5] When you've completed both sides, begin weaving the bottom of the frame with the thread left from step 3, or tie on a new piece. Weave the beads of row 45, which span from one edge of the warp to the other.

[6] Weave a row or two, then check overall alignment to make sure the inner corners of the frame form right angles. Adjust one side or the other if needed by pushing rows a bit closer together or spreading them slightly. You can't do this if you've split any warp threads on previous rows.

[7] Your weaving is done with row 57. Weave in all the thread tails and trim them. Leave the piece on the loom.

finishing warp ends

[1] Cut two strips of iron-on interfacing, each about 1 x 7 in. (2.5 x 18cm). Cut a second pair of strips measuring 1 x 5 in. (2.5 x 13cm).

[2] Center one of the long strips under the warp threads at one end of the piece with the adhesive side up. Fold the ends over the top to meet in the middle, cinching the outermost warp threads in slightly so they won't show when folded behind the beadwork (photo h).

[3] Use a pressing mitt underneath and press to seal the interfacing.

[4] Repeat at the other end. Then use the shorter strips to seal the warp threads inside the frame (photo i).

[5] Use scissors to cut the woven piece off the loom, cutting through the outer edge of the interfacing strips.

[6] Fold the interfacing strips to the back. Narrow them if necessary and press one on top of the other (photo j).

assembling the frame

[1] To assemble a photo frame with a leather back, subtract ¼ in. (6mm) from the finished width and height of the beadwork and cut out a backing piece of Foamcore or matboard that size.

[2] For the stand, cut a matboard piece 1½ x 3 in. (3.8 x 7.6cm). Then score and bend one end in about ¾ in. (2cm) from the end.

[3] Trace around the beadwork on a piece of leather or Ultrasuede. Cut a horizontal 1½-in. wide slit in the middle of the leather about 1¾ in. (4.4cm) up from the bottom. Push the folded part of the stand through the slit.

[4] Center and lightly glue the backing piece to the bottom portion of the wrong side of the leather. Don't apply glue above the slit. Insert the fold of the stand (photo k) and glue it and the top half of the leather to the rest of the backing.

[5] Use clothespins to clamp things in place and carefully whipstitch (Basics, p. 3) the leather to the edge of the beadwork on three sides (photo l). Insert the photo from the fourth side. Stitch the side closed if desired. ●

– *Jeanne Leffingwell*

Contributors

Claudia Cattell, originally from New Jersey, graduated from Ringling School of Art and Design in Sarasota, Florida. She has worked as a designer and senior art director in Hawaii and New York. Claudia currently writes and illustrates children's fables. She lives in Scottsdale, Arizona, with four Yorkshire Terriers, five horses, and seven birds.

May Flaum has been crafting for as long as she can remember. She experiments with new techniques in scrapbooking, altered arts, and home décor. May also enjoys teaching, reading, watching classic movies, and spending time with her husband and daughter. Visit her website at designsbymay.blogspot.com.

Denise Giles is a needlework and ribbon artist. Her passion for ribbon embroidery began more than 10 years ago; since then, she has had hundreds of designs published in magazines, books, and on the Web. Denise is a member of The Society of Creative Designers and The Craft & Hobby Association. She lives in East Texas, where her beautiful surroundings inspire much of her work.

Jeanne Leffingwell is nationally known for her architectural glass bead sculptures. She seeks to pass along the bead-working and craft techniques she has collected and learned all her life, beginning with her childhood in Alaska. Jeanne teaches in many communities in the Northwest, and is the founder of the Million Bead Project. She lives with her husband, guitarist James Reid, and their two children in Moscow, Idaho.

Lorine Mason has been a passionate crafter for most of her life. She designs using a variety of art mediums and maintains an open mind about each of her creative endeavors, resulting in one-of-a-kind pieces. She is a member of The Society of Creative Designers and The Craft & Hobby Association. She resides with her family in Herndon, Virginia.

Lesley Weiss is an assistant editor with Kalmbach Books.

Get Great Jewelry Projects All Through the Year

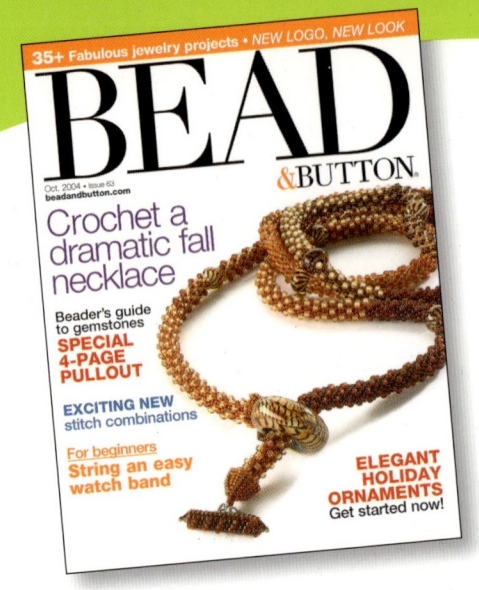

Your Beading Resource!

Bead&Button magazine
- New and traditional stitching techniques
- Fully-tested projects
- Step-by-step instructions and photos

Fast. Fashionable. Fun.

BeadStyle magazine
- Beautiful pieces in today's hottest styles
- Make jewelry in an evening or less
- Great photos and easy-to-follow instructions

If you enjoyed *Beaded Photo Frames* make sure you order these titles from the Easy-Does-It Series.

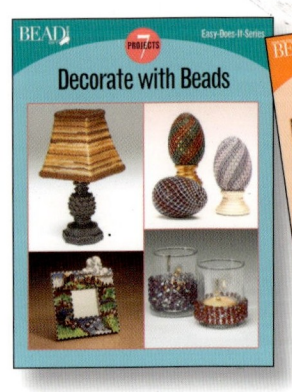

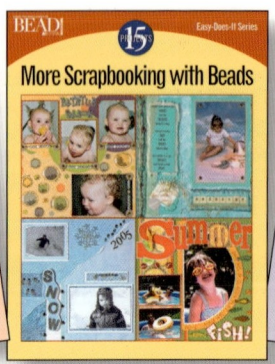

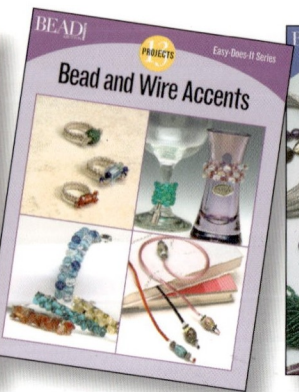

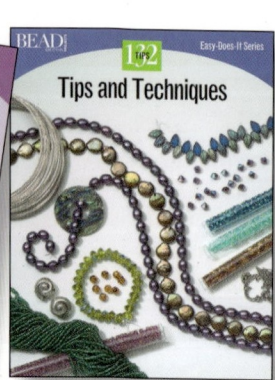

- Decorate with Beads
- Scrapbooking with Beads
- More Scrapbooking with Beads
- Bead and Wire Accents
- Tips and Techniques

Subscribe or Order Today and Enjoy New Beading Projects Every Month!
Call 1-800-533-6644 or visit
beadandbuttonbooks.com

KALMBACH PUBLISHING CO.

ISBN 0-89024-625-4 $7.95 U.S. 12316